RECORDED VERSIONS GUITAR

AUTHENTIC TRANSCRIPTIONS
WITH NOTES AND TABLATURE

Transcribed by JESSE GRESS

TIMEPIECES
THE BEST OF ERIC CLAPTON

14 AFTER MIDNIGHT

53 COCAINE

2 I SHOT THE SHERIFF

19 KNOCKIN' ON HEAVEN'S DOOR

61 LAY DOWN SALLY

35 LAYLA

93 LET IT GROW

78 PROMISES

85 SWING LOW SWEET CHARIOT

71 WILLIE AND THE HAND JIVE

27 WONDERFUL TONIGHT

104 Notation Legend

This publication is not for sale in
the EC and/or Australia
or New Zealand.

ISBN 0-7935-2210-2

HAL•LEONARD CORPORATION

7777 W. BLUEMOUND RD. P.O. BOX 13819 MILWAUKEE, WI 53213

I Shot The Sheriff

Words and Music by Bob Marley

3

for the life ___ of the dep - u - ty. ___ But I say, ___

I ___ shot the sher - iff, ___ but I swear it was in

self de - fense.

4

And ev - 'ry time _____ that I plant ___ a seed, ___ he

said, "Kill ___ it be - fore _____ it grows." _____ He

said, "Kill ___ it be - fore _____ it ___ grows." _____ I _____ say,

let ring - - - - - - -

Gtrs. 1 & 2   N.C.

6

Verse

3. Free-dom came my __ way __ one day, __

even bends

an' I start-ed out __ of town, __ yeah.

All of sud-den, I __ see sher-iff John __ Brown. __

aim-in' to shout me __ down, __ so I

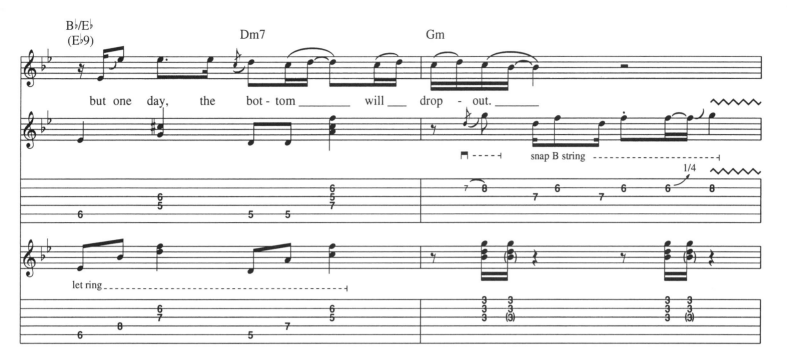

but one day, the bot-tom will drop-out.

snap B string

let ring

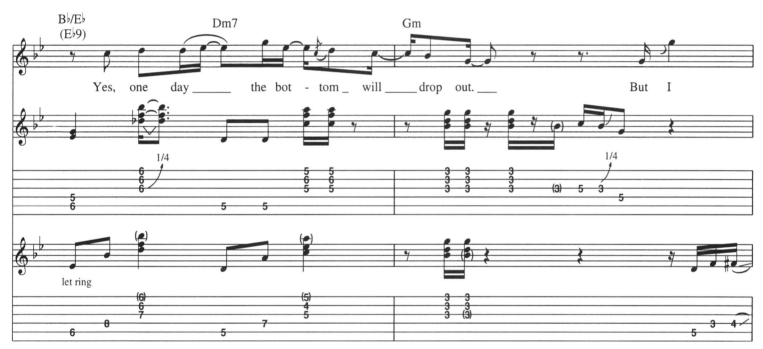

Yes, one day the bot-tom will drop out. But I

let ring

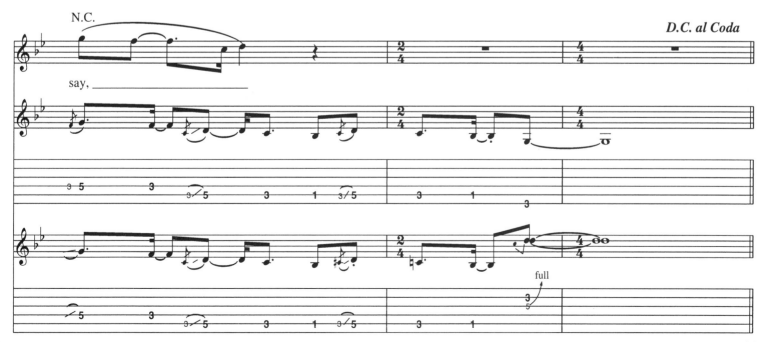

D.C. al Coda

N.C.

say,

full

Coda

Gm | Instrumental Bb/Eb | Dm7

dep - u - ty, _ oh __ no. ____

Instrumental Verse

Gm | Bb/Eb | Dm7

hold bend

Gm | Bb/Eb (Eb9) | Dm7

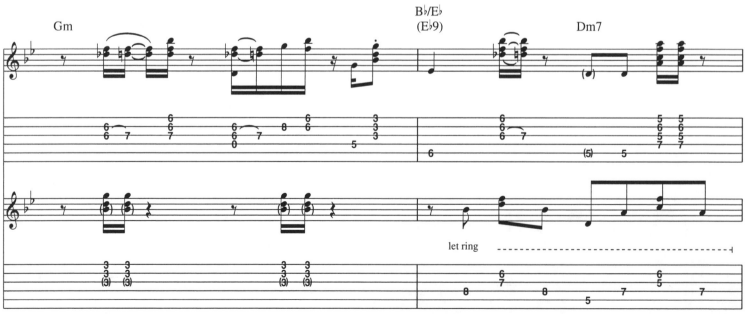

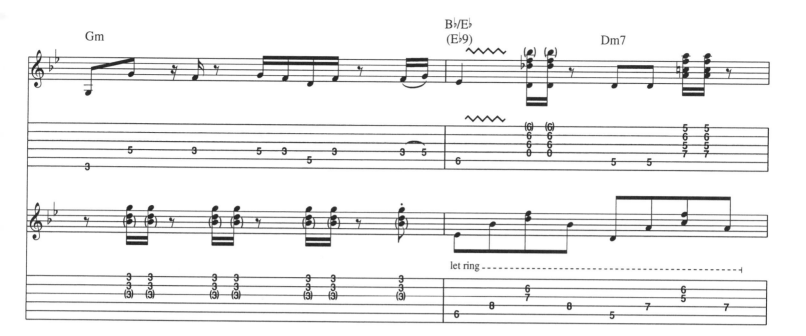

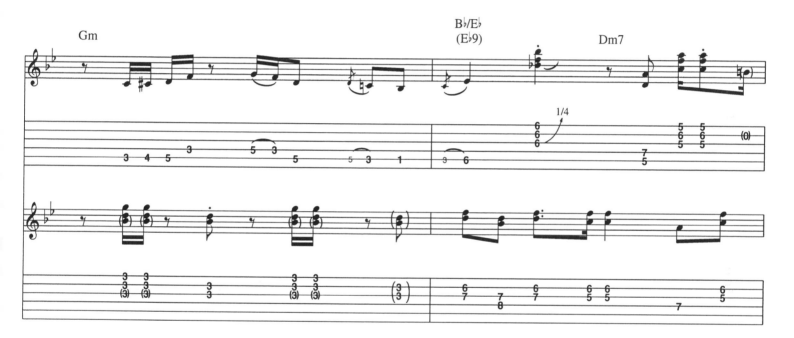

After Midnight

Words and Music by John J. Cale

Knockin' On Heaven's Door

Words and Music by Bob Dylan

Verse

w/Fill 1 (2nd verse only)

1.,3. Ma,   take this badge   off of   me.
2. Ma,   take these   guns away from me.

* Gtr. 2 plays strings ①,② of
1st verse voicings on 2nd and 3rd verse

Harmony tacet on 2nd verse

I can't use   it   an - y - more.
I can't shoot them   an - y - more.

Fill 1 Slide gtr.
(G tuning)

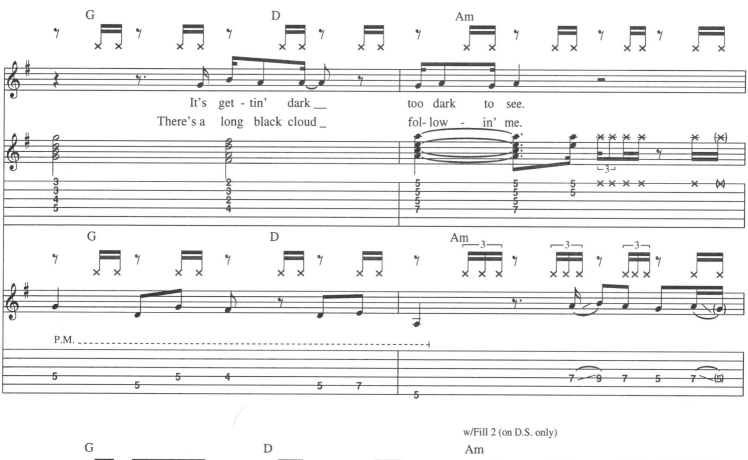

It's get-tin' dark __ too dark to see.
There's a long black cloud __ fol-low - in' me.

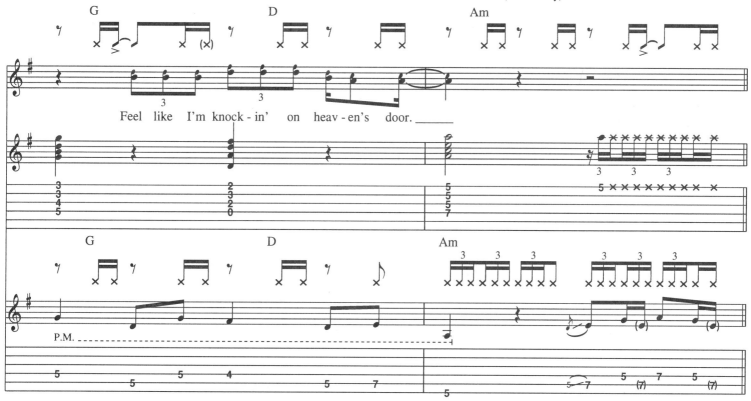

w/Fill 2 (on D.S. only)

Feel like I'm knock-in' on heav-en's door. _____

Fill 2

Slide gtr. (G tuning)

mf w/wah-wah   *even gliss*

Chorus

Knock, knock, knock-in' on heav-en's door. _____

w/wah-wah

P.M.

Knock, knock knock-in' on heav-en's door. _____

dim.

1st verse only

2nd verse only (P.M.)

(P.M.)

D.S. 𝄋 al Coda ⊕

Wonderful Tonight

Words and Music by Eric Clapton

Intro

Moderately w/half-time feel ♩ = 95

Bridge

I feel won - der - ful ___ be - cause I see ___ the love-

Gtr. 3 tacet

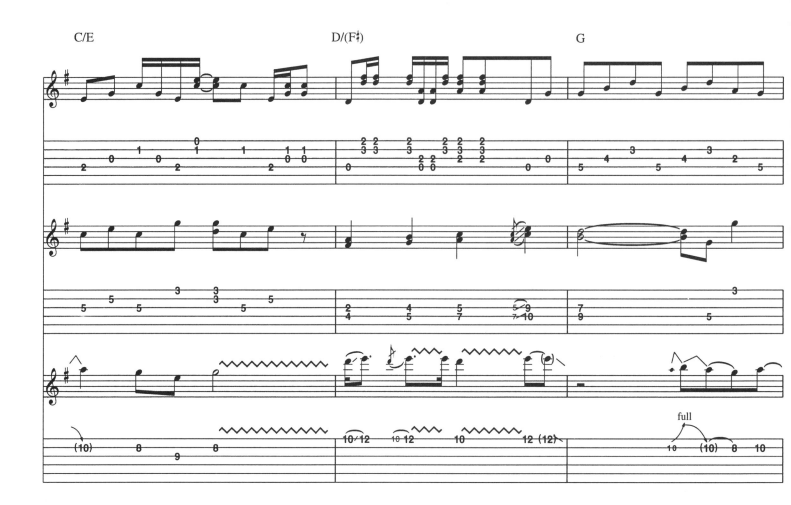

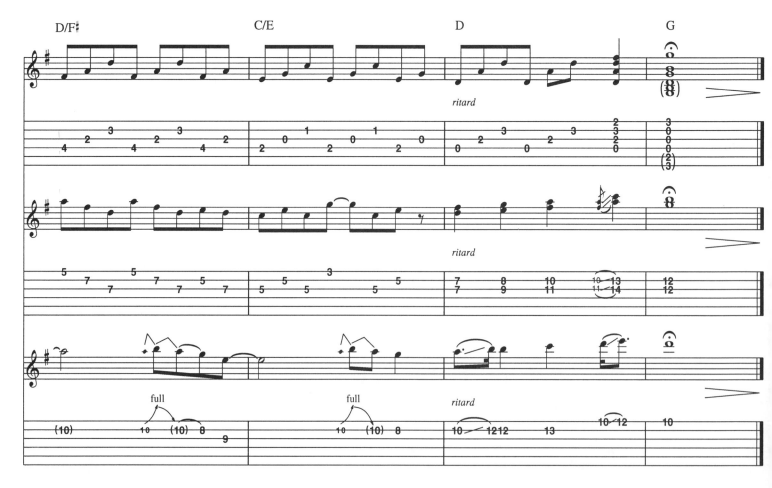

Layla

Words and Music by Eric Clapton and Jim Gordon

Chorus

All Gtrs. same as Section A

38

2nd Verse

2. I tried to give _ you con - so -la - tion   when your old man, _ he let _ you _

down. _   Like a fool, _____   I fell in love _ with you, _____

* Doubled as in intro.

Chorus

Slide Guitar Solo

Gtr. 3: w/Rhy. Fig. 1 (8 times)
Gtrs. 1, 2, 4 and 5 same as Section A (2 times)

N.C. (Dm)

* TAB numbers based on location
of notes beyond fretboard.

Gtrs. 1, 2, 4 and 5 same as Section A

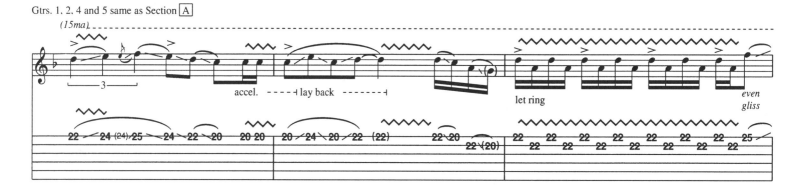

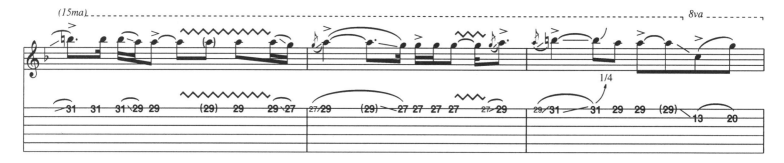

Gtrs. 1 and 2 w/Fill 5
Gtrs. 4 and 5 w/Fill 6

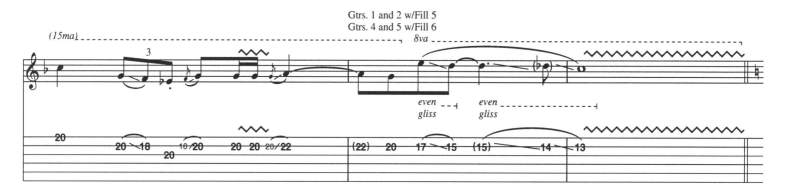

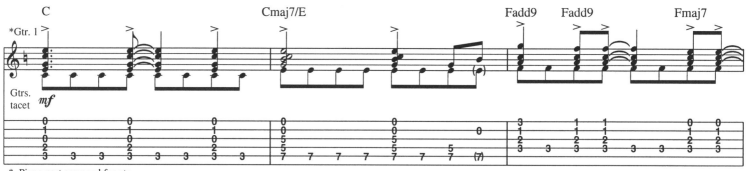

* Piano part arranged for gtr.
All gtrs. are re-numbered for the remainder of the song.

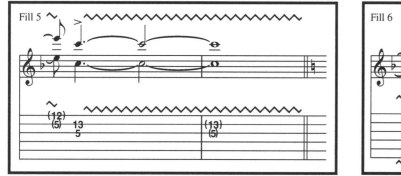

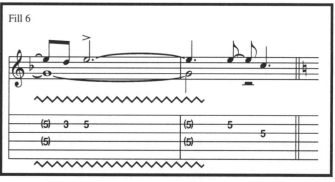

51

Piano arr. for gtr. ritards simile

Cocaine

Words and Music by John J. Cale

2. If you ___

Guitar Solo

even bend

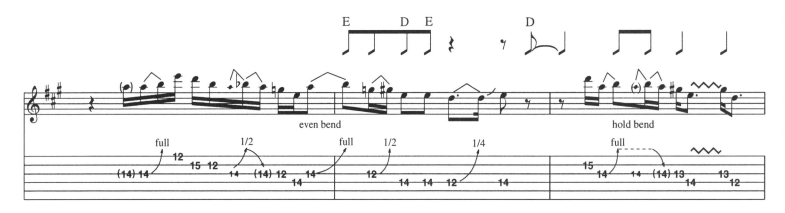

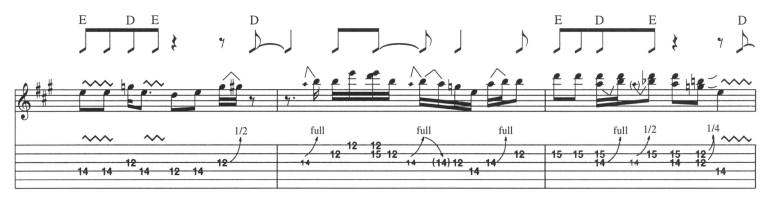

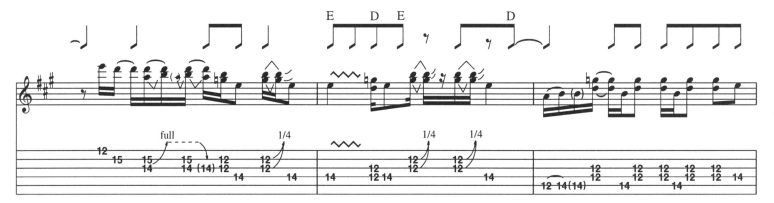

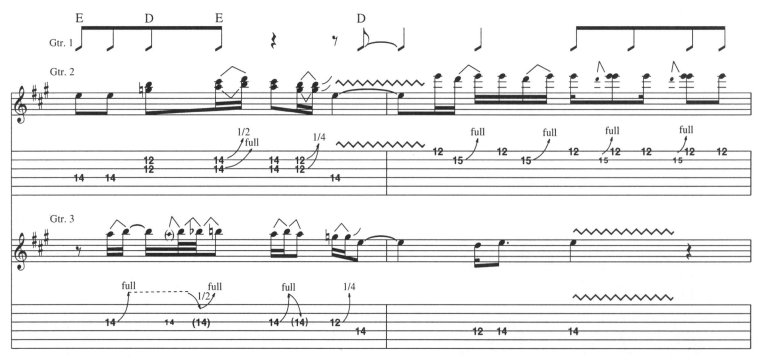

3. If your

she don't lie ___ she don't lie, ___ co- caine. ___

She don't lie, ___

Lay Down Sally

Words and Music by Eric Clapton,
Marcy Levy, and George Terry

2. The talk to you.____

Guitar Solo

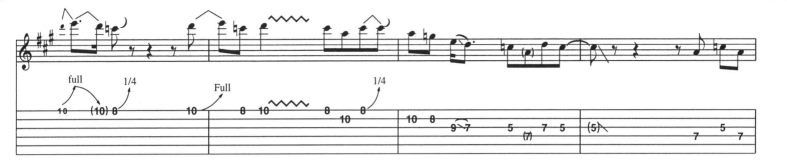

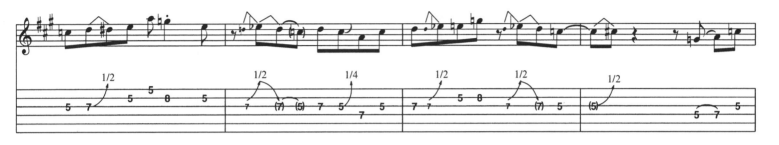

D.S. 𝄋 al Coda ⊕

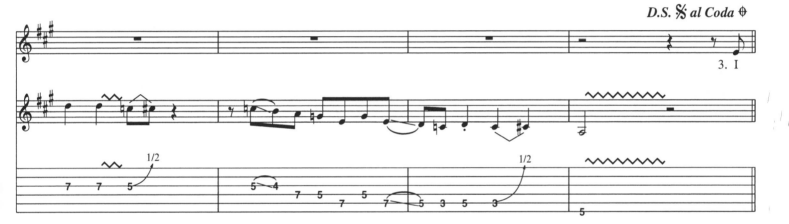

3. I

Coda
⊕

talk to you.___   **Chorus**   Lay_   down   Sal - ly   and

Instrumental Outro

Begin fade

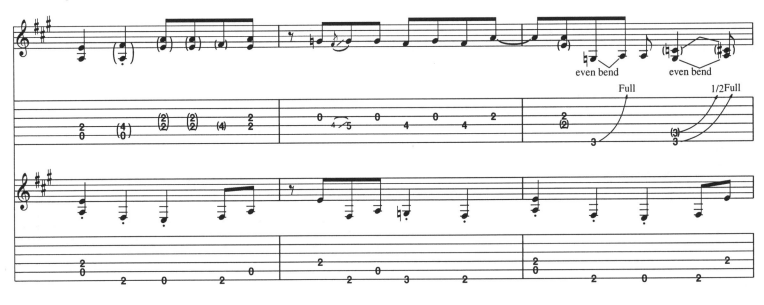

Fade out

Willie And The Hand Jive

Words and Music by Johnny Otis

Gtrs. simile on repeat

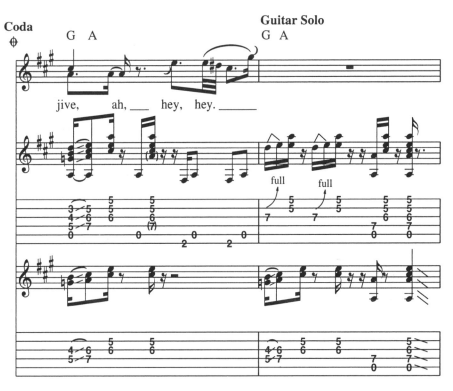

jive, ah, ___ hey, hey. _____

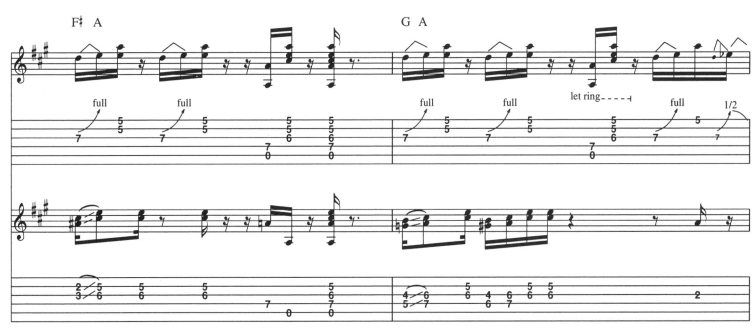

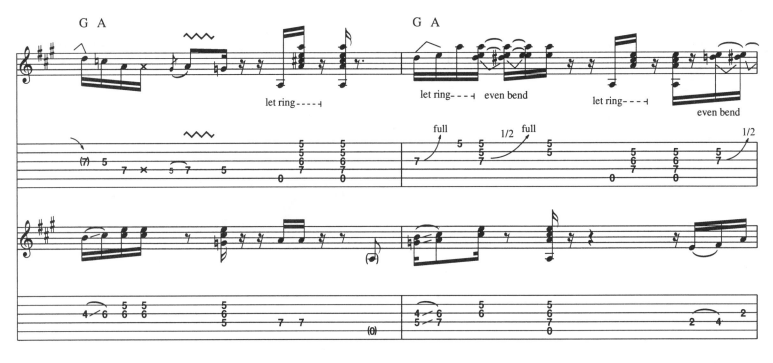

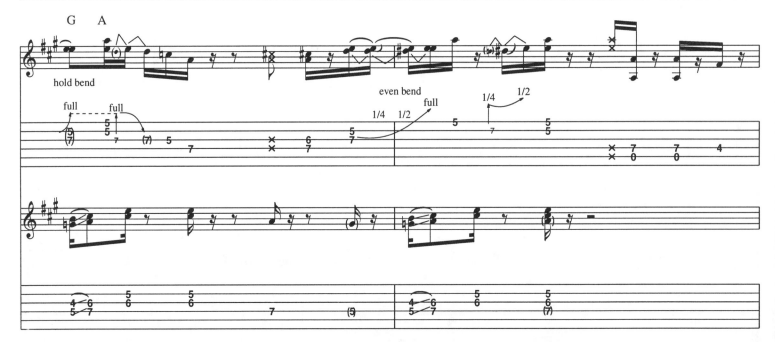

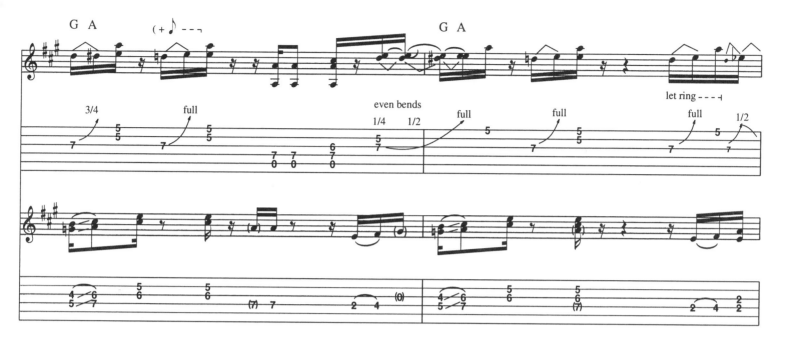

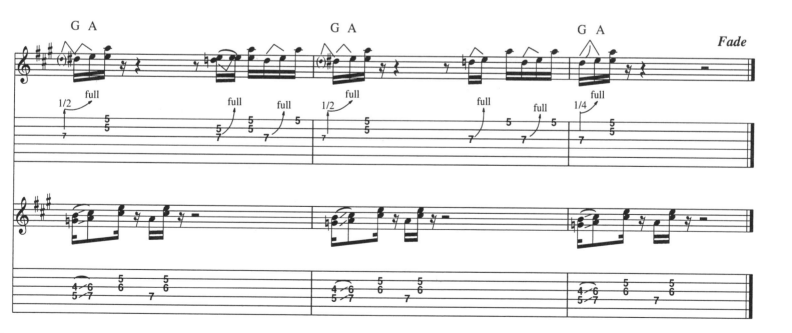

Promises

Words and Music by
Richard Feldman and Roger Linn

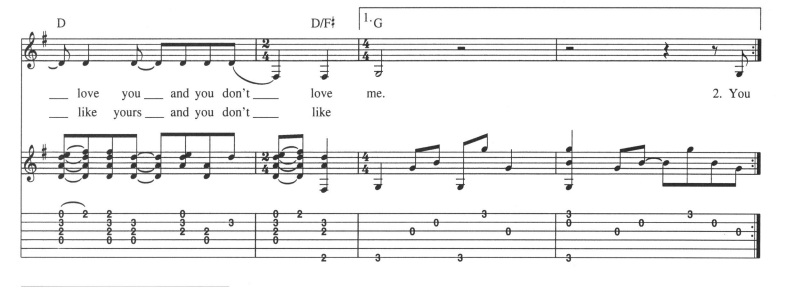

love you ___ and you don't ___ love me.   2. You
like yours ___ and you don't ___ like

mine.   La   la,   la la la ___ la ___

Elec. Gtr. 2
w/slide   Riff A

mf even gliss   even gliss

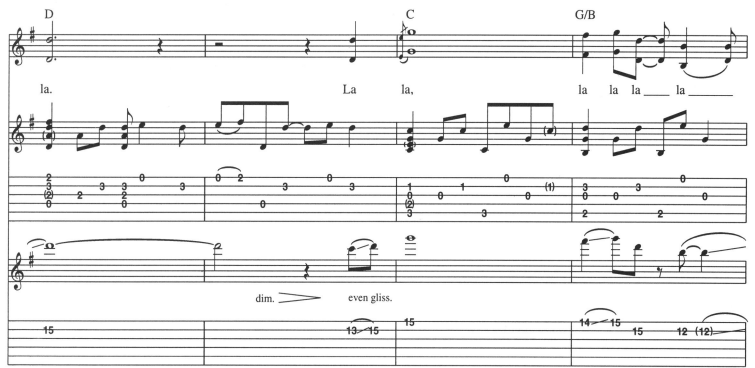

la.   La   la,   la la la ___ la ___

dim.   even gliss.

don't   love   you and you don't _____ love   me.
still   love   you if you'd just _____ love   me.

Chorus

I've got a prob - lem.   Can you re - late? ___
    I've got a prob - lem.   Can you re - late? ___

let ring throughout

I got a wom - an
    I got a wom - an   cal - lin' love

even gliss

81

*Dobro in open G tuning
⑥=D, ⑤=G, ④=D, ③=G, ②=B, ①=D

La   la,   la la la __ la ____ la.   Whoa, _____

Elec. gtr. 2
w/slide (cont. from Riff A)

Dobro repeats 4 bar pattern simile   *even gliss.*   *even gliss.*

Begin fade

Repeat and Fade

la,   la la la __ la ____ la.   Whoa, _____

Dobro repeats simile

even gliss.

Swing Low Sweet Chariot

Traditional, Arranged by Eric Clapton

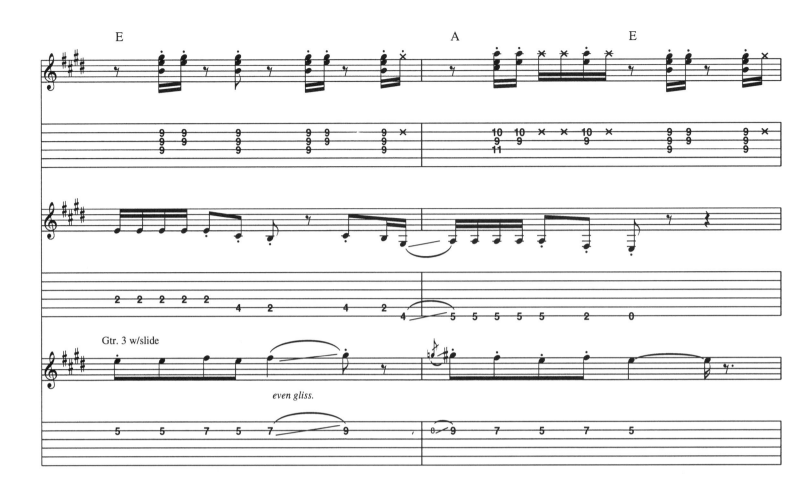

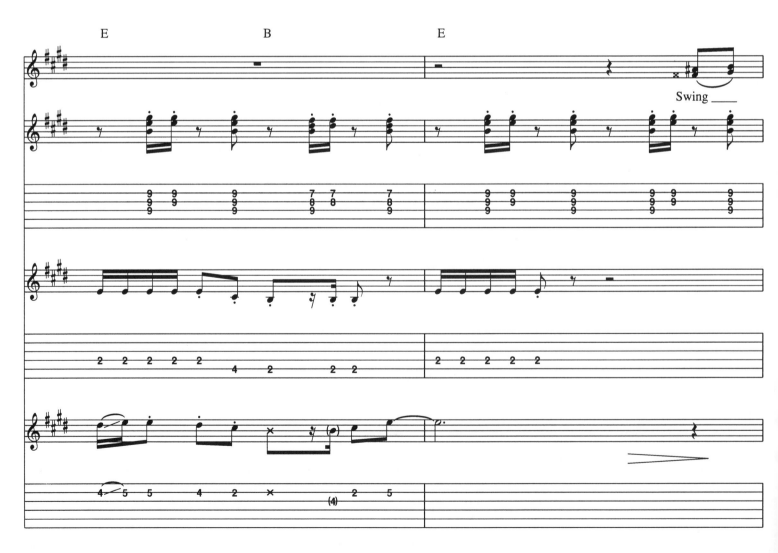

char - i - ot. ____ Com-in' for to car - ry me home.

2. I

home.

Guitar Solo

* Gtr. 3 w/slide

* Gtr. 3 in open E tuning.

P.H. Pitch: G C♯

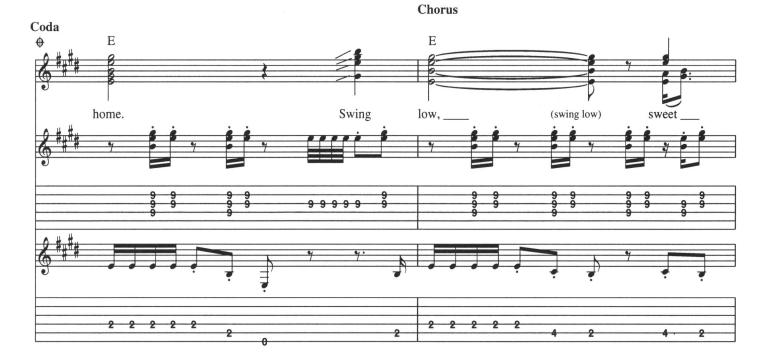

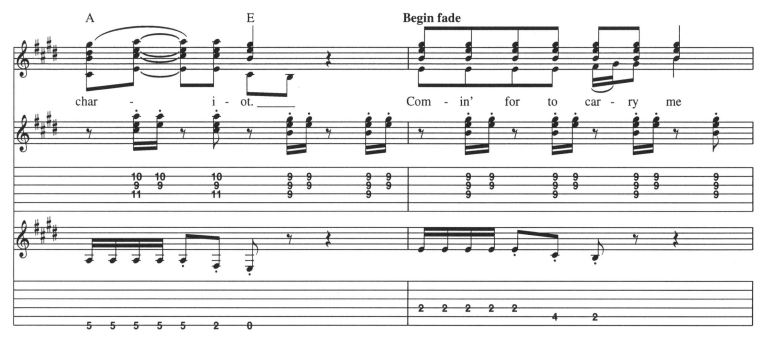

Let It Grow

Words and Music by Eric Clapton

let it blos-som let __ it flow.

In the sun, __ the rain, __ the

let arpeggio ring throughout

snow, _____

love is love - ly, __

let __ it

grow.

2. Look-ing for a rea - son   to check out   on my mind.

Interlude

96

* Bottom two notes of chord

NOTATION LEGEND